THEMATIC UNIT
Fairy Tales

Written by Jeanne King

Teacher Created Materials, Inc.
P.O. Box 1040
Huntington Beach, CA 92647
©1995 Teacher Created Materials, Inc.
Made in U.S.A.

ISBN-1-55734-246-6

Illustrated by
Agi Palinay and Jose L. Tapia

Edited by
Barbara M. Wally

Cover Art by
Blanca Apodaca La Bounty

Table of Contents

Introduction

Fairy Tales contains a captivating whole language, thematic unit. Its 80 exciting pages are filled with a wide variety of lesson ideas and activities designed for use with primary children. At its core are two high-quality children's literature selections, *The Jolly Postman or Other People's Letters* and *The Talking Eggs*. For each of these books, activities are included which set the stage for reading, encourage the enjoyment of the book, and extend the concepts gained. In addition, the theme is connected to the curriculum with activities in language arts (including daily writing suggestions), math, science (the study of sound), social studies, art, music, and life skills (cooking and physical education). Many of these activities encourage cooperative learning.

Suggestions and patterns for games and activities which feature familiar fairy tale characters and stories allow the students to synthesize their knowledge as they construct products that can be shared beyond the classroom. The culminating activity provides directions for a Fairy Tale Ball which merges a variety of activities to help children synthesize what they have learned. These features combine to make this book a very complete teacher resource.

This thematic unit includes:

- ❏ **literature selections**—summaries of two children's books with related lessons (complete with reproducible pages) that cross the curriculum

- ❏ **poetry**—suggested selections and lessons enabling students to write and publish their own works

- ❏ **planning guides**—suggestions for sequencing lessons each day of the unit

- ❏ **writing ideas**—daily suggestions as well as writing activities across the curriculum, including Big Books

- ❏ **curriculum connections**—in language arts, math, science, social studies, art, music, and life skills such as cooking and physical education

- ❏ **bulletin board ideas**—suggestions and plans for student-created and/or interactive bulletin boards

- ❏ **group projects**—to foster cooperative learning

- ❏ **a culminating activity**—which requires students to synthesize their learning to produce a product or engage in an activity that can be shared with others

- ❏ **a bibliography**—suggesting additional literature and nonfiction books on the theme

To keep this valuable resource intact so that it can be used year after year, you may wish to punch holes in the pages and store them in a three-ring binder.

Introduction *(cont.)*

Why Whole Language?

A whole language approach involves children in using all modes of communication: reading, writing, listening, observing, illustrating, experiencing, and doing. Communication skills are interconnected and integrated into lessons that emphasize the whole of language rather than isolating its parts. The lessons revolve around selected literature. Reading is not taught as a subject separate from writing and spelling, for example. A child reads, writes (spelling appropriately for his/her level), speaks, listens, etc., in response to a literature experience introduced by the teacher. In this way, language skills grow naturally, stimulated by involvement and interest in the topic at hand.

Why Thematic Planning?

One very useful tool for implementing an integrated whole language program is thematic planning. By choosing a theme with correlating literature selections for a unit of study, a teacher can plan activities throughout the day that lead to a cohesive, in-depth study of the topic. Students will be practicing and applying their skills in meaningful context. Consequently, they will tend to learn and retain more. Both teachers and students will be freed from a day that is broken into unrelated segments of isolated drill and practice.

Why Cooperative Learning?

Besides academic skills and content, students need to learn social skills. No longer can this area of development be taken for granted. Students must learn to work cooperatively in groups in order to function well in modern society. Group activities should be a regular part of school life, and teachers should consciously include social objectives as well as academic objectives in the planning. For example, a group working together to write a report may need to select a leader. The teacher should make clear to the students the qualities of good leader-follower group interaction and monitor them just as he/she would state and monitor the academic goals of the project.

Why Big Books?

An excellent, cooperative, whole language activity is the production of Big Books. Groups of students or the whole class can apply their language skills, content knowledge, and creativity to produce a Big Book that can become a part of the classroom to be read and reread. These books make excellent culminating projects for sharing beyond the classroom with parents, librarians, and other classes. Big Books can be produced in many ways. This thematic unit book includes directions for one method you may choose.

Why Journals?

Each day your students should have the opportunity to write in a journal. They may respond to a book, write about a personal experience, or answer a general "question of the day" posed by the teacher. Students should be encouraged to refer to the posted vocabulary list to check their spelling. The cumulative journal provides an excellent means of documenting writing progress.

The Jolly Postman or Other People's Letters

by Janet and Allan Ahlberg

Summary

The Jolly Postman comes one day with letters for the residents of a certain fairy tale countryside. As the postman rides through the countryside, he delivers letters, postcards, and catalogues to characters such as Red Riding Hood, B.B. Wolf, Esq., and Goldilocks. Each envelope holds a special surprise.

The outline below is a suggested plan for using the various activities that are presented in this unit. You should adapt these ideas to fit your own classroom situation.

Sample Plan

Day I

- Introduce writing activities, page 8.
- Complete "Fairy Tale Miles," page 42.
- Read the *Post Office Book* by Gail Gibbons.
- Choose city and street names, zip code and assign seat numbers, page 10.
- Make individual mailboxes, page 10.
- Address envelopes for letters, page 13.

Day II

- Continue writing activities, page 8.
- Begin making Jolly Postman book, pages 14–15.
- Write a return address, page 13.
- Write a letter to a classmate, page 13.
- Sequence mail from sender to receiver, page 16.

Day III

- Continue writing activities, page 8.
- Calculate Fairy Tale Postage, page 43.
- Make a pop-up greeting card, page 61.

- Map the Jolly Countryside, page 18.
- Make a "giant" giant, page 17.

Day IV

- Continue writing activities, page 8.
- Work on individual Jolly Postman books.
- Write a postcard from Snow White to the Seven Dwarfs, page 59.
- Make a jigsaw puzzle, page 60.
- Complete How Does Your Giant Measure Up? page 44.
- Make fairy tale graphs, pages 45–46.

Day V

- Continue writing activities, page 8.
- Read a Jolly map, page 57.
- Make tea using infusion, pages 48–49.
- Work on individual Jolly Postman books.
- Make scones for tea party, page 69.

Overview of Activities

SETTING THE STAGE

1. Prepare the classroom for a fairy tale unit. Enlarge the geometric shapes shown on page 63 to make a large castle for the bulletin board. At the top, label the board "Once upon a time ..." and at the bottom "happily ever after."

2. Discuss fairy tales. Which ones are they familiar with? Have they read them or seen the movies? Do they have any favorite characters or stories?

3. Begin setting up your classroom post office, using the ideas on pages 10–12.

4. Create a letter writing center (pages 74–77). Provide patterns for friendly and business letters, postcards and envelopes. Include fairy tale letterhead stationery, index cards to be used as postcards, stickers, and envelopes for students to use as they write to classmates or imaginary characters.

5. Brainstorm ways people can communicate their thoughts or feelings to each other (i.e., talking on the phone, sign language, writing letters, etc.).

6. Ask students about mail they have received. Do they write letters? Do they receive letters, magazines, or packages? Have students complete "Introducing the Jolly Mail" on page 9.

ENJOYING THE BOOK

1. Read *The Jolly Postman or Other People's Letters* or listen to the tape. Take out each letter, game, and card and allow children to examine each item.

2. Have children construct their own Jolly Postman books. As the unit progresses, assign a variety of items to be added to the books:

   - letters
   - pop-up greeting card
   - postcards
   - jigsaw puzzle

   Have the children address the envelopes to the appropriate character and insert their creations.

3. Ask students how they know which way to go. Have they ever used a map? Discuss directions and introduce major compass points. Teach the use of "Never Eat Soggy Waffles." Do "Mapping the Jolly Countryside" on page 18.

Overview of Activities *(cont.)*

ENJOYING THE BOOK *(cont.)*

4. Talk about how a post office works. How does the Jolly Postman get the mail to deliver? Students will come up with a variety of ideas. Do the sequencing activity on page 16.

5. Continue creating a classroom post office on pages 10–12. Have the children make their own mailboxes, adding their desk numbers and street names. Assign classroom post office jobs and have the children write letters to each other.

EXTENDING THE BOOK

1. Read a variety of fairy tales like the ones listed in the bibliography. Compare the main elements of these fairy tales, using "A Fairy Tale Recipe" on page 19.

2. Do the "Hansel and Gretel Summary" on page 38 to illustrate the use of the five W's in summarizing a story. Divide the story into three segments.

3. Do the "Gingerbread House" art project on page 39 or 61 to create a fairy tale cottage. If space permits, display the completed cottages to form a village.

4. Use simple geometric shapes to create "Cinderella's Castle" on page 63. Use the completed castle as the cover for fairy tales written or drawn by the students.

5. Make a classroom fairy tale cookbook. Use the handout and parent letter on page 78 to request recipes. Add the recipes on pages 69 –70 to those contributed by students and make copies for each child. Use the fairy tale castle or the gingerbread house on page 39 to make covers and have children decorate them.

6. Do the art activity on page 17 and the measurement activity on page 44.

7. Have students graph their favorite fairy tales on a classroom chart on pages 45–46.

8. Plant Jack's beanstalk and measure its daily growth on pages 50–52.

9. Write a cooperative fairy tale, using elements on page 19 and frame on page 30. Children can illustrate it to make a Big Book. Have the children write and illustrate their own fairy tales to add to your Big Book, or bind the individual stories and put them in a special section of your classroom library to be used for silent reading.

10. Have a tea-tasting party. Use the infusion experiment on pages 48–49. Make one of the scones recipes on page 69 in class.

11. Read *The Post Office Book: Mail and How It Moves* by Gail Gibbons.

12. Team up with an upper/lower grade class to exchange letters from fairy tale characters (i.e., sixth grade students—B.B. Wolf, Esq., third graders—Little Pigs or their attorney).

Daily Writing Topics

1. Rewrite *Jack and the Beanstalk* from the giant's point of view.

2. What happens after "happily ever after"? Choose a fairy tale and tell what happens in the next five years.

3. Summarize the story of *Hansel and Gretel*. Write no more than three sentences for each section, telling the major events of the beginning, the middle, and the end. Remember to cover the five W's. (See page 38.)

4. Red Riding Hood is having a birthday party and you are invited. Describe who else is there, the games you play, and the presents she receives.

5. Read a Grimm's fairy tale and do a book report on it.

6. You are a reporter covering the events that happened in a fairy tale. Write a newspaper article, using the five W's (who, what, when, where, why or how).

7. A giant came into the classroom last night. Why did he come? What did he do? Why did he leave? Teacher preparation: Cut six or seven large footprints and place them around the classroom for the children to find when they enter in the morning.

8. Write an apology note from Goldilocks to the Three Bears.

9. Your ruler is a magic wand. What do you do with it?

10. One day a man/woman appears before you and says she/he is your fairy godmother/father. Which three wishes does he/she grant you and what do you do with them?

11. You are trapped overnight in a castle. Who locked you in? Why? What happens?

12. Write a letter from Cinderella to her ugly stepsisters and stepmother.

13. On the way back to the castle, Prince Charming is kidnapped by a dragon. Snow White has to save him. How does she do it?

14. Make up an eighth dwarf. Tell his story.

Introducing the Jolly Mail

Soon we will be learning about some special letters and the way that mail is delivered.

Do you like to write letters? _____

To whom did you write your last letter ?

_____

How many letters do you write to friends or relatives in:

    one week? _____

    one month? _____

    one year? _____

List three people you would like to write letters to:

_____   _____   _____

Do you like to receive letters? _____

From whom did you last receive a letter? _____

How many letters do you receive from friends or relatives in:

    one week? _____

    one month? _____

    one year? _____

Have you ever received something other than a letter by mail? _____

    Postcards? _____   How many in a year? _____

    Magazines or newspapers? _____   How many in a year? _____

    Packages? _____   How many in a year? _____

Classroom Post Office

Set up a classroom post office in your room. Your students should select a city name and a zip code for your classroom. Make up a large city welcome sign to hang in the classroom.

In cooperative learning seating arrangements, each group of four to five children will choose a street name for their group and design a street sign to display above their group.

Each child will then be assigned a seat number. After these selections are made, each child will make a mailbox, using paper bags and the directions below. Have each student mark his/her seat number on it in large block letters.

Make a Mailbox

Materials:

- 1 paper bag for each student (Lunch bags work well.)
- red construction paper
- single hole punch
- pronged paper brads
- double-sided tape

Directions:

1. Students write their street numbers on one side of the bag. If they want, they may add their names and other decorations to their "mailboxes."

2. Cut strips of red construction paper 4" x 1" (10 cm x 2.5 cm). Make a hole 1" (2.5 cm) from one end.

3. Attach paper strip to bag with the brad as shown.

4. Using double-sided tape, mount each mailbox to the desk, making sure that the address and flag are on the outside.

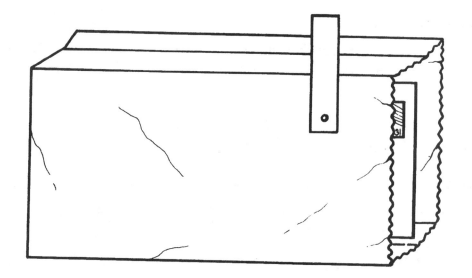

To Use

When mail is delivered, the postman raises the "flag," so that student knows he/she has received mail. A student may raise his/her flag to alert the postman mail needs to be picked up.

Classroom Post Office *(cont.)*

Central Post Office

Place a box with a lid in the classroom. It can be decorated to look like a real mailbox, but it should have a slot for mail and a lid for easy removal of mail. Transfer the pattern on page 12 to construction paper and paste to the box to create a mailbox.

Classroom Jobs

These jobs can be switched each week to allow each child a chance to understand the workings of a post office.

Job Descriptions

Mail Carriers (two) pick up mail daily from the mailbox and deliver it to the Central Post Office. At the end of each day, they pick up outgoing mail at the Central Post Office and deliver it to the individual addresses.

The Postmaster or Postmistress sorts mail daily, cancels stamps, bundles the mail according to street address, and has it ready for the Mail Carrier pick up.

Mail Sorting

Set up a file or cubbyhole for each child (cardboard shoe organizers are excellent). Arrange their files in groups according to street names.

Note: You may wish to provide the following items to make your Post Office more "official."
- hats for Mail Carriers and Postmaster/Postmistress
- large book bags labeled Jolly Mail

Classroom Post Office *(cont.)*

Mailbox Pattern

Transfer pattern and color to make a class mailbox.

12

Sending Jolly Mail

Give each student an envelope or, if you wish, use the pattern on page 75 to make envelopes. Have each child address it to him/herself using classroom addresses.

Kerry King
2 Beanstalk Road
Giant City, CA 91709

Pick up these envelopes and exchange them with students seated at the other streets. The second student then puts his/her classroom address as the return address on the envelope.

Jason Calvert
4 Fairy Tale Lane
Giant City, CA 91709

Kerry King
2 Beanstalk Road
Giant City, CA 91709

This child will now write a letter to the person to whom the envelope is addressed, design a stamp for the letter, and place it in the mailbox when finished.
Mail Carriers will pick up mail and deliver it to the Central Post Office (designated in classroom).

The class Postmaster and Postmistress will cancel stamps on incoming mail, then sort the mail and bundle it according to street names.

Mail Carriers will take the bundled mail from the Central Post Office and deliver it to the addressees. See page 10 for individual mailbox pattern.

Extension:

Set up a letter writing center with a chart showing the main parts of a letter and envelope address form. Have paper, stickers (to be used as stamps), and envelopes on hand.

These letters can be mailed, sorted, and delivered daily.

Alternate the roles of Mail Carriers and Postmaster/Postmistress so that each student has a hands-on experience with each phase of the process.

Make a Jolly Postman Book

You will enjoy writing your own Jolly Postman books. Use the pattern on page 15 and the directions below to create your books. When you are finished, share them with the class.

Materials:
- envelope pattern (page 15)
- one 8" x 10" (20 cm x 25 cm) sheet of construction paper, cut in half lengthwise to form front and back covers
- a paper punch
- yarn, ribbon, or paper brads for binding

Directions:

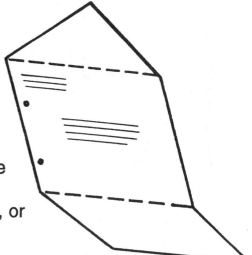

1. Cut out the envelope pattern.
2. Fold the pattern on the dashed line, making sure that the address lines are on the outside, and glue or paste the right edges together.
3. Add the front and back book covers.
4. Using the circles as a guide, punch holes in the envelopes and covers.
5. Fasten covers and envelopes with ribbon, yarn, or brads.

The envelopes are now ready to address to a favorite fairy tale character and fill with letters, postcards, or games.

Some Suggested Activities:
- Write a postcard from Snow White to the Seven Dwarfs, describing life in the castle, and illustrate it. (page 59)
- Make a fairy tale jigsaw puzzle. (page 60)
- Design a pop-up greeting card to a character (e.g., a get well card to Red Riding Hood's grandmother from the Wolf) on page 61.
- Send a birthday party invitation to one of the fairy tale characters.
- Write a letter from the Giant's lawyer to Jack.
- Send an advertisement to a character. For example, send a housewares sale flier to The Three Bears.
- Make up a bill for the Giant to send to Jack.

Make a Jolly Postman Book *(cont.)*

Name _____ Date _____

Delivering the Jolly Mail

Color the pictures, then cut them apart. Paste them on a sheet of paper to show the right order. Read the story.

1. The letters go through a machine that cancels the stamps so they cannot be used again.

2. The Mail Carrier picks up the mail and takes it to the Central Post Office.

3. The Jolly Postman takes the mail from the Central Post Office and delivers the mail to the Three Bears' cottage.

4. Goldilocks mails a letter to The Three Bears.

5. The Three Bears read Goldilocks' letter and sit down to write her an invitation to tea.

6. The letters are sorted by zip code and then by street names. (A truck takes the mail for other zip codes to other post offices.)

Extension: On the back of the paper, draw pictures to show what happens to the Bears' letter.

Make A "Giant" Giant

This creative project will get the students working cooperatively and will allow for cross-curricular extensions to enhance their experience.

Divide the class into four equal groups and assign a number to each group. Give each person a large piece of butcher paper with instructions to construct only the assigned body part (e.g., 1's make the head, 2's make the torso, 3's make the legs and feet, and 4's make the arms and hands). Brainstorm creative ways to make the parts more interesting.

When they finish with their art work, assemble giants from the pieces. You now have several whimsical giants to hang about the room.

Mapping the Jolly Countryside

When following a map, the Jolly Postman remembers his directions by using this phrase, "Never Eat Soggy Waffles." The top of a map is always north, so beginning at the top the N in "Never" stands for north, the E in "Eat" stands for east, the S in "Soggy" stands for south, and the W in "Waffles" stands for west.

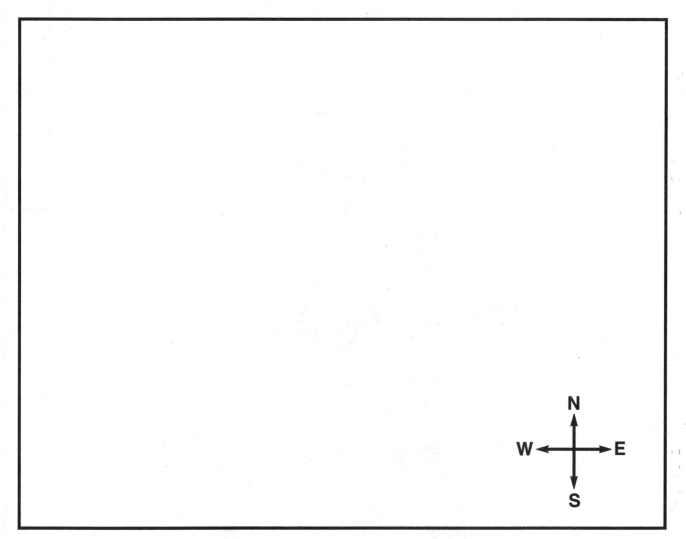

Follow the directions:

1. Draw the Witch's gingerbread house in the northern section of your map.
2. Draw Jack's beanstalk in the southern part of your map.
3. Draw Red Riding Hood's flower garden in the western section of your map.
4. Draw the Big Bad Wolf in the eastern part of your map.

Bonus:

Write two more directions on the back of this page. Give them to a friend to complete. Remember "Never Eat Soggy Waffles."

A Fairy Tale Recipe

Most fairy tales have many elements in common. These elements are listed below. Create a chart of stories and elements as shown below and post it in the classroom. As stories are read, discuss them and fill in the chart. Children should be able to pinpoint which elements apply to each story or character. By learning to synthesize this information, the children should be able to apply these elements in writing their own fairy tales.

	Jack and the Beanstalk	Red Riding Hood	The Three Little Pigs	Hansel and Gretel	The Three Bears	The Talking Eggs
The fairy tale begins "Once upon a time…"						
The fairy tale happens long ago and far away.						
Some characters are royalty.						
Some characters are good; some are evil.						
There is a problem to solve.						
Someone makes a plan to solve the problem.						
There is some magic in the fairy tale.						
Something happens in threes.						
Someone gets a reward.						
There is a "happily ever after" ending.						

The Talking Eggs

by Robert D. San Souci

Summary

The Talking Eggs is adapted from a Creole folktale published in the late nineteenth century. It appears to have its roots in popular European fairy tales, which were probably brought to Louisiana by French emigres.

Blanche lives with her sister Rose and mother on a poor Southern farm. Sweet Blanche does all of the work while her sister and mother put on airs and dream of being rich.

One day Blanche is sent by her mother to the well for water, and there she meets a magical old woman who rewards the child's good heart and obedient attitude with riches found in the "talking eggs." This story reveals a classic plot line where good is rewarded and evil is punished.

The outline below is a suggested plan for using the various activities in this unit. You may need to adapt the plan to meet the needs of your particular class.

Sample Plan

Day I

- Begin writing activities, page 23.
- Read *The Talking Eggs*.
- Complete "Egg Word Problems," page 47.
- Explore sound with sight, page 55.

Day II

- Continue writing activities, page 23.
- Discuss similes and complete activity sheet, pages 24–25.
- Begin writing a cooperative fairy tale, page 30.
- Conduct an experiment to feel sound, page 56.

Day III

- Continue writing activities, page 23.
- Write "I'm As . . ." poems, page 26.
- Learn to do "Egg Logic," page 28.
- Design a magic egg and write a story about it, page 27.
- "Can Eggs Really Talk?," pages 53–54.

Day IV

- Continue writing activities, page 23
- Write a wishing well story, page 33.
- Learn about symmetry, page 29.
- Create musical instruments, pages 66–68.
- "Fairy Tale Ball" culminating activity, pages 72–73.

Overview of Activities

SETTING THE STAGE

1. Display a variety of decorative eggs. Different sizes of plastic eggs are usually available in craft stores, or use blown eggs.

2. Discuss eggs with the children. Are all eggs the same? Where do eggs come from? Do they use eggs at home?

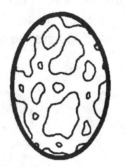

3. Select an egg and tell students that it is a magic egg. Hold it to your ear and act as though the egg is saying something to you. Ask the children what they think the egg might be saying.

4. Pass the egg around and encourage the children to imagine that this is really a talking egg and to share what the egg said to them.

5. Ask if eggs can really talk.

6. Write a class story about the egg. Encourage children to use elements from the Fairy Tale recipe to tell about the egg and its special powers.

ENJOYING THE BOOK

1. Show students the cover of *The Talking Eggs*. Ask them to predict what they think it might be about based on the title and the pictures.

2. Read *The Talking Eggs* for enjoyment. Pause at appropriate moments and ask children to predict what will happen next. Allow students to examine the details in each picture, and discuss them.

3. Use the fairy tale recipe on page 19 to compare this story to other fairy tales.

4. To encourage critical thinking, discuss the following:

   • Do you think you would have done what Blanche did? Why or why not? Why do you think Blanche was able to control herself so well?

   • What about Rose? Did not following orders make her a bad person?

   • Why or why not?

Overview of Activities *(cont.)*

ENJOYING THE BOOK *(cont.)*

5. Discuss the use of similes in the book. Ask children if they have ever heard similes used. Some common similes may prompt them to contribute others—"Hungry as a horse," "Quiet as a mouse," "Growing like a weed." Make a list on the chalkboard or on a large sheet of paper. Use the handouts on pages 24–25 to have the children illustrate what they think the author meant with his use of similes.

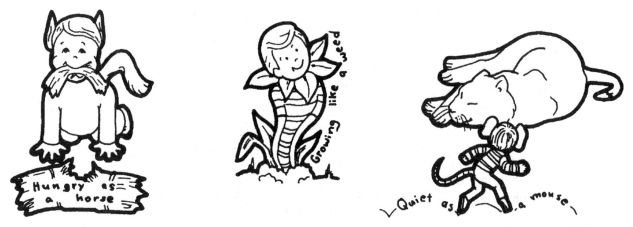

6. Have students sit quietly and close their eyes. Instruct them to listen carefully. The teacher stands at the back of the room and makes a variety of sounds—rattling paper, tapping on a desk, etc. Ask students to describe what they heard. Can sound be seen or felt? Begin sound study on page 55.

EXTENDING THE BOOK

1. Talk about major and minor characters, setting, and the major problem of the story. Make a character mobile, using the handout on page 62.

2. Make a Big Book of the "I'm As . . ." simile poems (page 26) to add to your classroom library.

3. Have the students write their own stories about finding a talking egg. What did it say? What did they do with it? Use the handout on page 27 and have students decorate the outside.

4. Use the cinquain pattern and directions on pages 31–32 to have children write about sounds. Substitute things that make sounds for the subject (e.g., thunder, rain, wind) and make lists of adjectives and verbs related to sound.

5. Use the Using Sound to Create a Classroom Band handouts on pages 66–68 to explore sound and how it works. Have the band play at the Fairy Tale Ball culminating activity.

6. Teach the children the Virginia Reel and other simple square dances to perform at the Fairy Tale Ball (see bibliography for references).

7. Play the recording of *Peter and the Wolf* by Prokofiev. Listen to the sounds and discuss how the sounds show the characters. Add the story parts to Fairy Tale Recipe chart, and compare it to other fairy tales.

Daily Writing Topics

1. You take a trip through an enchanted forest. You realize that this forest is a strange and silly place. Describe your trip and the strange sights and sounds you see (e.g. birds meowing, purple trees, etc.).

2. The forest animals are having a party, and you are invited. What happens?

3. Tell a story about the funniest thing you have ever seen.

4. Design your own magic egg. What powers does it possess? What causes its magic?

5. You come across a well in the forest. It is a magic wishing well. What wishes would you make?

6. Describe a time you did not follow a parent's instructions. What happened? What did you learn?

7. Pretend you are Blanche and write a thank you note to the old woman for the talking eggs.

8. Imagine you are at a party with Blanche. Describe the guests and their costumes.

9. Choose a color. Describe all the real, imaginary, and magical things it reminds you of.

10. Write a fairy tale with you as the hero/heroine. What big problems must you solve? How do you try to solve them? Are you successful?

11. Pretend to be one of the characters from *The Talking Eggs* and tell what has happened to you since you met with, or learned of, the old woman.

12. The old woman had many strange animals. Create your own unusual animal by using parts of two or more common animals. For example, you may have a cat that barks or a dog that flies. Remember to make your animal colorful, and tell how it is useful. Exchange your description with a partner, and try to draw each other's animals.

13. Write a story about being lost in the woods. Describe the colors you see and the sounds you hear. Tell why you are there. Does anyone or anything you find there help you? How? Remember to use the five W's in telling your story.

Similes

In *The Talking Eggs,* the author uses similes to create pictures in the reader's mind. Similes use the words *like* or *as* to compare objects or people in order to show similarities (e.g., pretty as a picture, strong as an ox).

Below are some of the similes used in *The Talking Eggs.* In the frame next to the simile, draw what you think the author meant.

1. **"They lived on a farm so poor; it looked *like* the tail end of bad luck."**

2. **"Blanche was sweet and kind and sharp *as* forty crickets."**

3. **". . . they were alike *as* two peas in a pod."**

Similes *(cont.)*

4. "A cow with two heads, and horns *like* corkscrews, peered over a fence..."

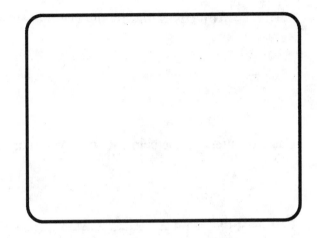

5. "These chickens didn't cluck, but whistled *like* mockingbirds."

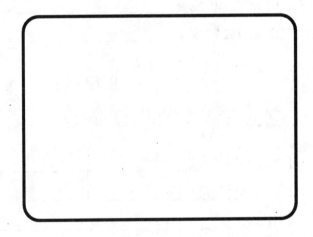

6. "The old woman . . . took off her head. She set it on her knees *like* a pumpkin."

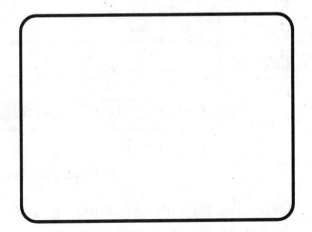

"I'm As..."

Brainstorm a list of nouns and adjectives on the board. Have the children use the patterns below to create their own simile poems.

Adjectives (*describing words*)   **Nouns** (*naming words*)

Use the pattern frame below to write your simile poem to show all the different ways you are you.

I'm As...

I'm as quick as a_____ .   I'm as slow as a _____ .

I'm as large as a _____ .   I'm as small as a_____ .

I'm as loud as a _____ .   I'm as quiet as a_____ .

I'm as lazy as a_____ .   I'm as busy as a _____ .

Put them all together and you've got me!

I'm As...

I'm as _____ as a_____ .

I'm as _____ as a_____ .

I'm as _____ as a_____ .

I'm as _____ as a_____ .

I'm as _____ as a_____ .

I'm as _____ as a_____ .

I'm as _____ as a_____ .

I'm as _____ as a_____ .

I'm as _____ as a_____ .

Put them all together and you've got me!

Extension for older students: In a revision of one of their creative writing projects, ask the children to incorporate one or two similes in their descriptions.

An "Eggstraordinary" Story

Design a special egg with magical powers. Write a story about it. How did you find it? What magical powers did it possess? What did it allow you to do? Write your story on the lines below, then cut out the top. Fold the paper on the dashed lines and decorate the outside of your egg to show how special it is.

Egg Logic

Note to Teacher: Give each child different color counters to represent each of the characters. Have them lay these counter across all four squares beside the character's name. As the students eliminate possibilities, the marker is removed until only one remains, and the answers become clear. As an alternative, have children use a crayon or pencil to place an "X" over eliminated possibilities. Ask questions to guide the reasoning process.

- Do birds sleep in caves, under a bush, or in rabbit burrows?
- Which places are best described as close to the ground?

Once an answer has been determined, it is no longer a possibility for other questions and should be eliminated.

Student Activity

Goldilocks and The Three Bears are hunting for eggs in the forest. See if you can use the clues below to find out where each character found his or her egg.

1. Mama Bear did not find her egg in the cave or under a bush.

2. Papa Bear found his in a place where birds sleep.

3. Goldilocks found hers close to the ground.

	Tree Hollow	Cave	Near the Rabbit's Burrow	Under a Bush
Papa Bear				
Mama Bear				
Goldilocks				
Baby Bear				

28

Egg Symmetry and Patterning

Symmetry means that a picture or an item is balanced. An equal number of items are on each side. The egg pattern below is incomplete. Extend the pattern from the left side to create a symmetrical pattern on the egg.

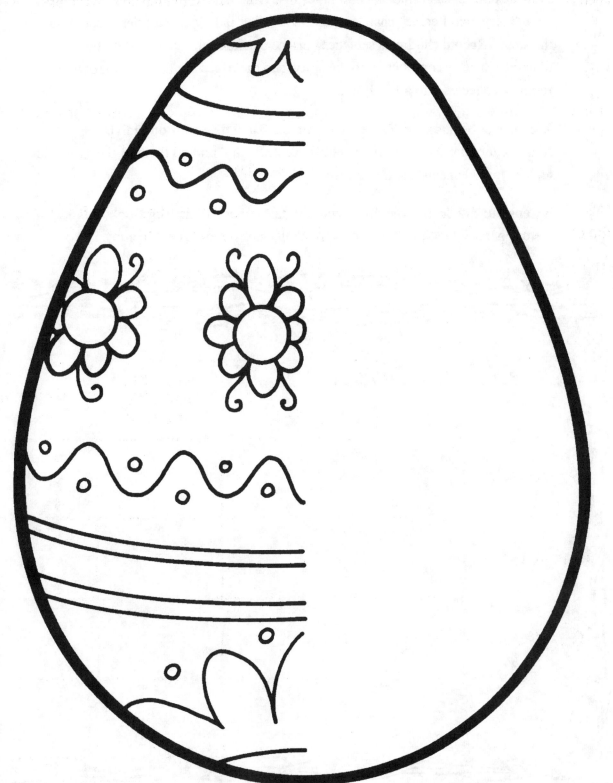

Write a Class Fairy Tale

In this exercise, each student contributes to a class fairy tale. Use questions based on a "Fairy Tale Recipe" chart on page 19 to elicit individual responses and guide the story. Record children's sentences on the chalkboard. Each student then illustrates his/her contribution to the story, and the pages are displayed around the room or collected into a Big Book.

The teacher begins with "Once upon a time…" and then calls on individual students for contributions. If students have difficulty, remind them of the fairy tale recipe story elements and the five W's.

Extension: Students write their own fairy tales to add to the Big Book or bind them separately and place on a class reading shelf for everyone to enjoy.

Once Upon a Time…

Write a Fairy Tale Cinquain

A cinquain is a five-line poem which contains the following lines:

> **Line 1** One word which names the subject.
>
> **Line 2** Two words which describe or define the subject.
>
> **Line 3** Three words which tell what the subject did.
>
> **Line 4** Four words about what happened.
>
> **Line 5** One word that sums up, restates, or supplies a synonym for the subject. Sometimes it is considered a free line.

In addition to reviewing stories and characters, this activity can be used to introduce or review nouns, adjectives, verbs, and synonyms.

1. Read the cinquain "Almost Gingerbread." Display it on the chalkboard or make a poster of it so that children can refer to it as they work.

Almost Gingerbread

Hansel
Clever and Kind
Following white pebbles
Finds the gingerbread house
Yum! Yum!

2. Have children brainstorm names of characters in the stories they have read. Use the first line of the cinquain as an example and list the suggestions on a piece of 12" x 18" (30 cm x 45 cm) construction paper. These will provide subjects for the cinquains.

3. Discuss adjectives or describing words. Use a second piece of construction paper to list as many adjectives as children can brainstorm which describe fairy tale characters.

4. On a third sheet of paper, list action words to be used in line three and four.

5. Finally, make a list of words associated with the endings of fairy tales to end the cinquain.

Hang all the lists in the order they will be used for the cinquain. Explain that *cinq* is French for five, and each poem has five lines. Provide students with copies of the following page and allow them to write their own cinquains about a character or situation in a fairy tale. Completed poems can be read to the class, displayed, or bound into a Big Book.

Older children will not only be able to follow the word pattern but may also want to include the syllable or beat count, as shown in the following examples.

> **Title**—the major problem in the story
>
> **Line 1** A noun (2 syllables)
>
> **Line 2** Adjectives that describe the character (4 syllables)
>
> **Line 3** What the character did in the story (6 syllables)
>
> **Line 4** Phrase about what happened (8 syllables)
>
> **Line 5** Free line (2 syllables)

Extension: Use sounds as the subject of a cinquain poem. Generate lists of things that make sounds like thunder, rain, wind, traffic, etc. Make lists of appropriate adjectives and verbs, following the procedures above.

Name _____

My Fairy Tale Cinquain

_____

noun
(the subject)

_____ _____

adjective **adjective**
(describing word) (describing word)

_____ _____ _____

verb **verb** **verb**
(action word) (action word) (action word)

_____

four word phrase
(about the subject)

_____

free line
(summary or restate)

The Magic Wishing Well

Blanche meets the old "aunty" at the well. Imagine you come across a magic wishing well.

"Think about" the following questions:

- What wish would you want granted?

- Why do you want it?

- Why would getting your wish make you happy?

- Who would you share your wish with?

- How would your life change with your wish?

Now, write a story on the wishing well about how your wish came true.

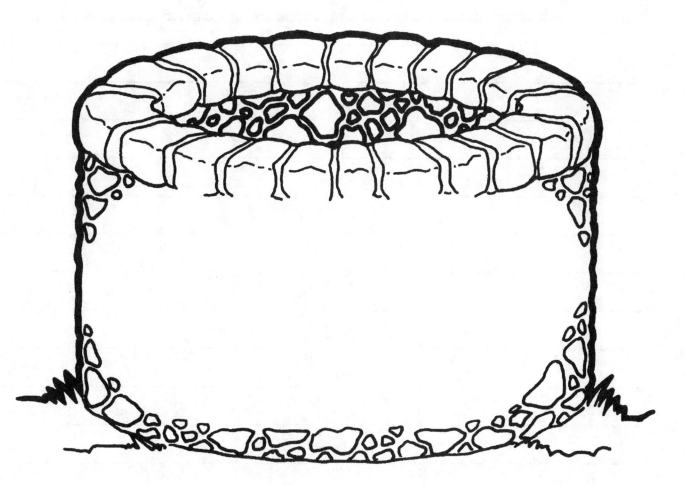

Fairy Tale News

Choose a fairy tale and write a newspaper article about the events that took place in it. Choose a headline from those below (or make up your own) and use the reporter's five W's to tell about the event. Work in groups or as a class to make a newspaper.

Boy Grows Giant Beanstalk!

Prince Charming to Wed

Snow White Wakes Up

Breaking and Entering at Bears' Cottage

Lost Children Return From Woods

Mystery Thief Robs Giant

Jack and the Beanstalk
Reader's Theater

Narrator 1: Once there lived a mother and her son, Jack. They were very poor.

Mother: Jack, we have no money. Take our cow to town and sell her, so we can eat.

Narrator 2: Jack had not gone far when he met an old man.

Old Man: Young man, where are you going?

Jack: I'm on my way to town to sell our cow.

Old Man: I have a bag of magic beans. They will give you great riches. I'll give them to you for your cow.

Narrator 1: Jack took the beans from the old man and ran home to show his mother.

Jack: Mother! Mother! Look! I sold our cow for these magic beans!

Mother: Jack, you stupid boy! You traded our cow for these worthless beans!

Narrator 2: With that, she threw the beans out of the window. The next morning, Jack looked out of the window and saw a huge beanstalk that reached far into the clouds. He rushed outside and began to climb it.

Narrator 1: After a long time, he reached the top of the beanstalk and saw a strange land sitting atop the clouds. Nearby was a great castle. Jack was hungry, so he knocked on the castle door. (Knock, knock, knock!) The giant's wife opened the door.

Jack: Please, may I have something to eat? I am very hungry.

Giant's Wife: Well, all right. But don't let my husband, the Giant, find you here. He just loves to eat little boys.

Narrator 2: Jack was eating quietly when he suddenly heard the Giant coming.

Giant: Fee, fi, fo, fum! I smell the blood of an Englishman. Be he alive, or be he dead, I'll grind his bones to make my bread.

Giant's Wife: Quick, hide!

Jack and the Beanstalk
Reader's Theater (cont.)

Narrator 1: Jack hid in the oven.

Giant: Wife! Bring me my dinner!

Narrator 2: The Giant ate his meal loudly. Then, he called to his wife.

Giant: Bring me my magic hen!

Narrator 1: The Giant's wife brought the hen and set it on the table.

Giant: Lay, hen, lay!

Narrator 2: As Jack watched, the hen laid an egg of gold on the table. When Jack saw the wonderful hen, he knew the hen was his father's that had been stolen long ago.

Narrator 1: After a time, the Giant went to sleep. Jack crept out from his hiding place and grabbed the hen. He ran back to the beanstalk and climbed down. The next day, Jack went up the beanstalk again. He knocked on the door. (Knock, knock, knock!)

The Giant's wife answered the door.

Jack: Please, may I have something to eat?

Giant's Wife: You again? I let you in last night, and you repaid me by stealing my husband's magic hen. Off with you now! I'll not let you in!

Narrator 2: Jack pretended to go away, but, instead, he sneaked inside the castle and hid.

Giant: Fee, fi, fo, fum! I smell the blood of an Englishman. Be he alive, or be he dead, I'll grind his bones to make my bread!

Giant's Wife: You only smell your dinner cooking. Eat your fill.

Narrator 1: The Giant ate his meal. Then he called to his wife.

Giant: Bring me my bags of silver and gold!

Narrator 2: Jack watched the Giant count his treasure and waited until he had fallen fast asleep. Then Jack took the bags and raced down the beanstalk.

Narrator 1: The next day, Jack climbed up to the castle and hid again. When the Giant came home, he yelled.

Jack and the Beanstalk Reader's Theater *(cont.)*

Giant: Fee, fi, fo, fum! I smell the blood of an Englishman! Be he alive, or be he dead, I'll grind his bones to make my bread!

Giant's Wife: There's no Englishman here. You must smell that boy you ate last Tuesday. Here's your dinner. It's all ready.

Narrator 2: The Giant ate his meal and then called to his wife.

Giant: Bring me my magic harp!

Narrator 1: The Giant's wife brought the magic harp and set it on the table.

Narrator 2: The harp began to play beautiful music, and soon, the Giant fell asleep. Jack took the harp and started to run to the beanstalk. But the harp cried out to the Giant.

Harp: Help, master, help!

Narrator 2: The Giant woke up and ran after Jack. Jack raced down the beanstalk with the Giant behind him.

Narrator 1: As soon as Jack reached the ground, he grabbed an ax and chopped the beanstalk down. The Giant fell to the ground, crashing through the earth and disappearing into a great hole.

Narrator 2: Jack and his mother now had the hen, the gold and silver, and the magic harp. So, from then on, they lived . . .

All: Happily ever after!

Hansel and Gretel Summary

After reading *Hansel and Gretel,* have the children write and illustrate a three-part summary booklet of the story. This lesson will teach the basic elements of summarizing a story effectively using the five W's (who, what, when, where, why or how) and emphasize the need to retell what happened in the beginning, middle, and end of the story.

Use the brainstorming sheet below to summarize the main elements of this story. Children will then transfer this information into a three-paragraph essay, which can be written in booklet form, using the gingerbread cottage pattern on the following page.

For each cottage book, provide each student with a cover page. (See page 39.) Cut lined paper to fit cottage shape and give each student three pieces.

Beginning:

Who (is the story about)? _____

Where (did the story take place)? _____

When (did this story happen)? _____

What (happened during the beginning of the story)? _____

Why or How (does the action take place)? _____

Middle:

Who (were the main characters in this part of the story)? _____

Where (is this part of the story taking place)? _____

When (does it take place—after that, after a while, the next day, etc.)?

_____

What (were the main things that happened in this part of the story)?

_____

Why or How (does the action take place)? _____

End:

Who (are the main characters in this part of the story)? _____

Where (is this part of the story taking place)? _____

When (does it happen—after a while, suddenly, two weeks later)? _____

What (happens in this section of the story)? _____

Why or How (is the problem solved)? _____

Gingerbread House Pattern

Story Pyramid

Teacher's Note: Summarizing a story can be difficult for children.

This story pyramid is an eight-line summary which provides an effective way to reduce the detail students tend to add to their summaries.

Directions:

1. Name of main character
2. Two words describing the main character
3. Three words describing the setting
4. Four words stating the problem
5. Five words describing one event in the beginning of the story
6. Six words describing one event in the middle of the story
7. Seven words describing one event at the end of the story
8. Eight words describing the solution to the problem

Example:

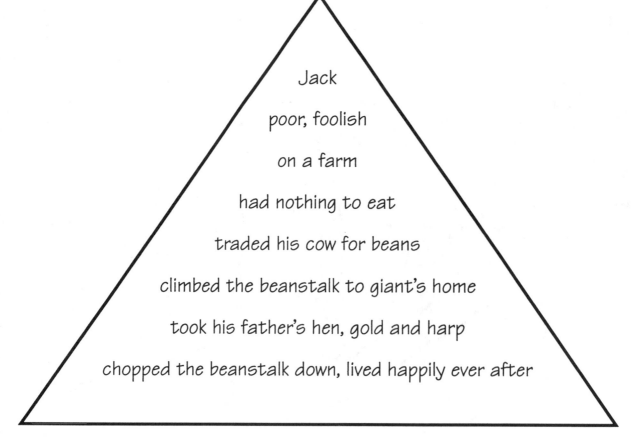

Jack

poor, foolish

on a farm

had nothing to eat

traded his cow for beans

climbed the beanstalk to giant's home

took his father's hen, gold and harp

chopped the beanstalk down, lived happily ever after

Now choose a fairy tale and make your own pyramid on page 41.

Name _____

My Story Pyramid

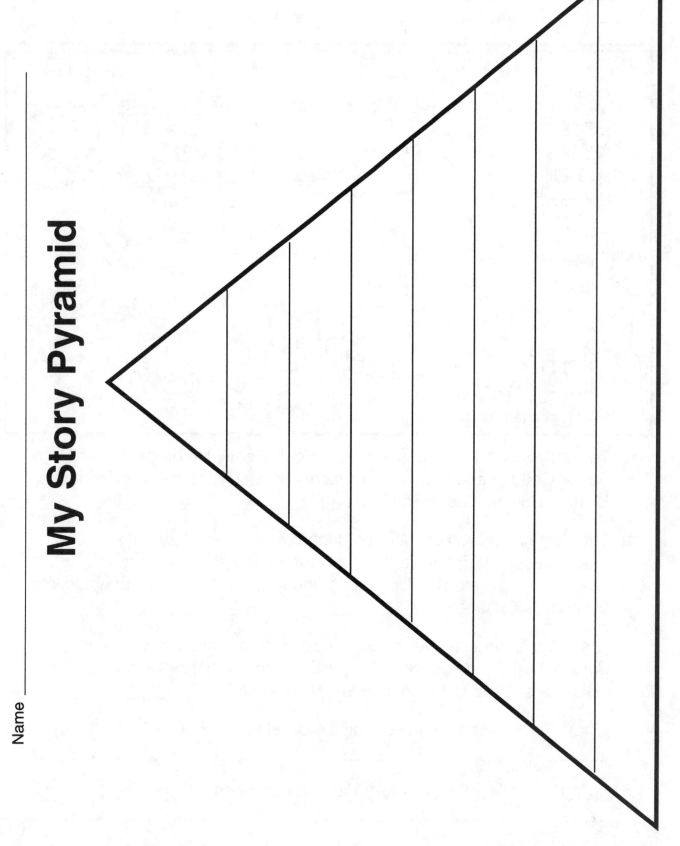

Fairy Tale Miles

The Jolly Postman delivers mail throughout the woods to our favorite fairy tale characters. Use the map to show how far he travels.

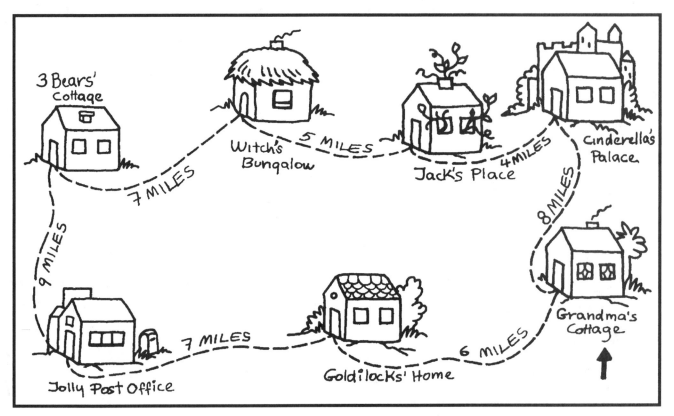

1. The Jolly Postman starts at the Jolly Post Office. He drops the mail at the Bears' Cottage and rides to the Witch's Bungalow. She asks him to stop for tea. How far has he traveled? _____

2. The Postman leaves the Witch's Bungalow, delivers the mail at Jack's Place, waves at Cinderella (no mail today), and stops to chat with Grandma. How many miles has he ridden from the Witch's Bungalow to Grandma's Cottage? _____

3. The Jolly Postman arrives at Goldilocks' Home and sees a letter for Cinderella. He rides back to the palace. How far does he ride from Goldilocks' Home to the Palace and back again? _____

4. What is the distance from Grandma's Cottage to the Jolly Post Office?

_____

5. How many miles does the Jolly Postman travel on his mail route?

_____

Fairy Tale Postage

Every letter, postcard, or package needs a stamp to be delivered from one place to the next. The chart below shows how much stamps cost at the Jolly Post Office. Use the chart to figure out the word problems below.

ITEM	COST
Letter stamps	$0.12
Postcard stamps	$0.10
Packages	$1.25

1. Cinderella is sending a package and a letter to her ugly stepsisters. How much will it cost to mail them?

_____

2. The giant sends 7 postcards to the Seven Dwarfs' Cottage. What will he pay for the stamps?

_____

3. Goldilocks is sending each of The Three Bears an invitation to tea. She needs 3 letter stamps. How much will she pay to mail her invitations?

_____

4. The Wicked Witch has sent a letter to each of these characters: Hansel, Gretel, Snow White, and Red Riding Hood. How much postage did she pay?

_____

5. Jack spent $0.22 on mail today. What did he buy?

_____

6. The Jolly Post Office sold 6 letter stamps, 4 postcard stamps, and postage for 2 packages on Monday. What was the total cost to send mail on Monday?

_____

Bonus:

How much do stamps cost at your post office?

How Does Your Giant Measure Up?

Assign a giant to each group. Each child will estimate his/her giant's measurements. Then, working in their groups, the children use a metric tape measure to find the exact measurements.

How Does Your Giant Measure Up?

First estimate (guess) your giant's measurements. Next, with your group, use a tape measure to find the exact measurements.

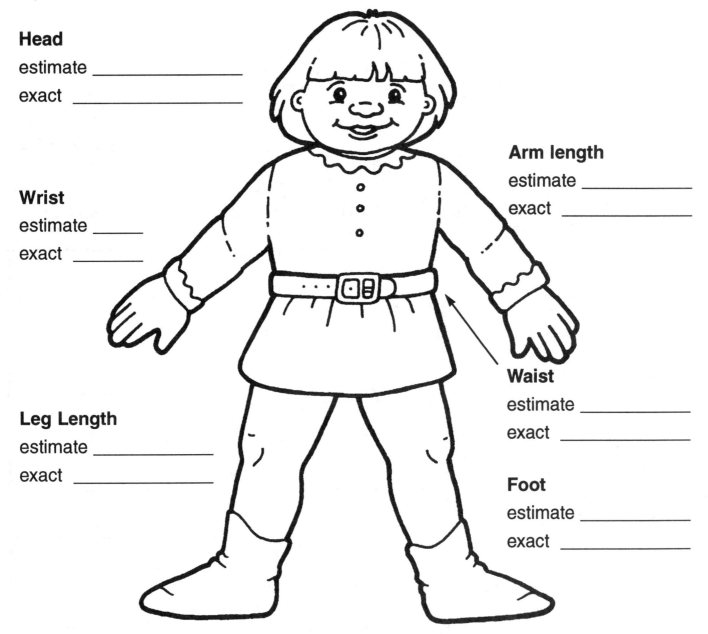

Head

estimate _____

exact _____

Wrist

estimate _____

exact _____

Arm length

estimate _____

exact _____

Waist

estimate _____

exact _____

Leg Length

estimate _____

exact _____

Foot

estimate _____

exact _____

Writing Extension:

Write a story about the giant that visited your room. Why was he here? What did he do while he was here? Where did he go afterwards?

Graph Your Favorite Fairy Tale

After your class has read through the following fairy tales, have them graph which is their favorite on a classroom chart like the one below. Other graphing activities are listed below.

1. How many more children chose _____ than _____ ?

2. How many fewer children chose _____ than _____ ?

3. How many children chose _____ and _____ all together?

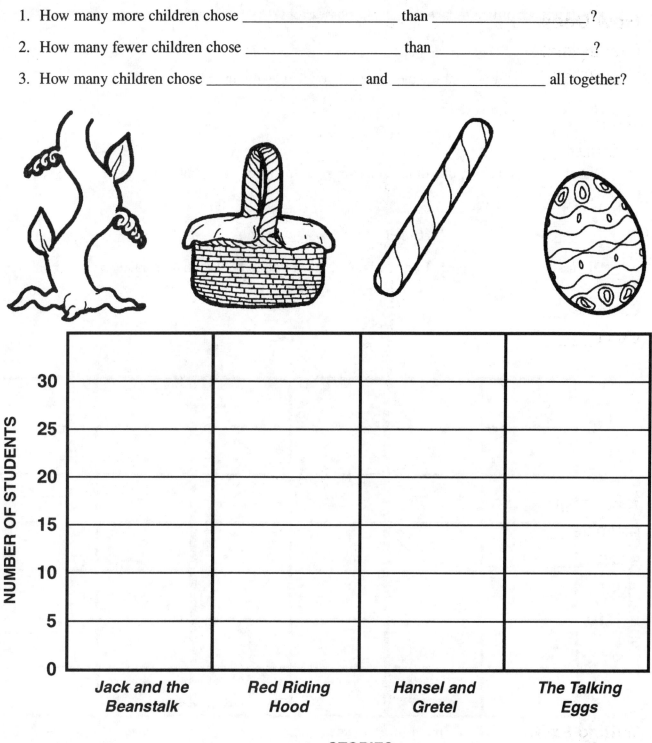

Graphing Activities

These questions should lead to some excellent discussions after your reading. Make a bar graph for each question as shown below to organize the data (responses).

1. Did Jack have a right to take the Giant's possessions?

   _____ Yes   _____ No

   Discussion—Why? What did the story tell you that lead you to believe that?

2. Have you ever disobeyed a parent?

   _____ Yes   _____ No

   Discussion—Tell about that time. Is it ever right to disobey an adult? A parent?

3. Who was more clever?

   _____ Hansel   _____ Gretel

   Discussion—Cite examples from the book that led you to believe that character was more clever.

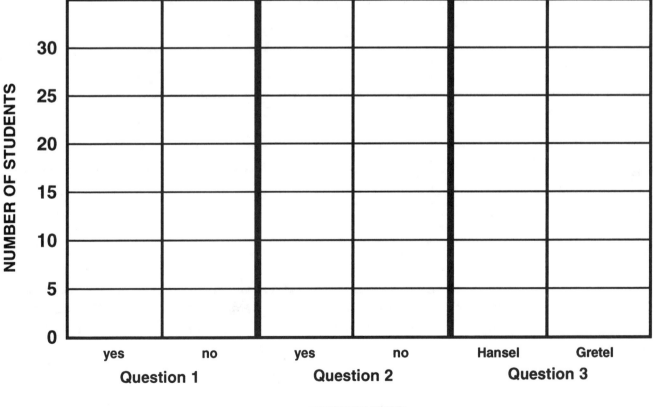

Egg Word Problems

During her trip to the old woman's cabin, Blanche saw many strange and wonderful sights. She may have seen many of these odd things below. See if you can use your number sense to figure out the answers to the problems below.

1. Chickens of every color came running to Blanche. There were four pink ones, six blue, seven yellow, and three polka dot ones. How many chickens were there all together?

2. Twelve rabbits played the banjo, 12 played the fiddle, and 12 rabbits danced to the music. How many rabbits were at the party?

3. There were 13 jeweled eggs and 23 plain ones in the henhouse. How many eggs were in the henhouse?

4. Blanche had 14 diamonds by the time she got home. She gave 5 to her sister. How many did she have left?

5. When Rose got to the henhouse, there were 28 eggs in there. Rose took 14 of them. How many were left?

6. Ten rabbits were walking in the cakewalk and three sat down. How many were still in the cakewalk?

Making Jolly Tea

When some solids are soaked in liquid, especially hot liquid, they change the liquid, or give it new qualities. This is called an *infusion*. Two common infusions prepared in the kitchen are coffee and tea.

Tea is made from an infusion of water, a liquid, with tea leaves, a solid. When the Jolly Postman stops by the homes of his fairy tale friends along his postal route, he is served this infusion.

In this experiment, you will discover some of the many other leaves and plant parts that can make drinks and learn the best conditions for extracting them.

How Do Solids Flavor Water to Form Tea?

Materials and Equipment:

teaspoons
2 tea balls or strainers
teakettle
water
paper and pencil
hot water cups

whole spices:
allspice (dried berries)
anise (seeds)
cinnamon (bark)
cloves (buds)
fennel (seeds)

herbs (leaves):
basil
marjoram
mint
oregano
rosemary
sage

Procedure:

Put about ¼ teaspoon (1.25 mL) of an herb or spice in the tea ball or strainer for each cup of "tea." Pour fresh boiling water into one cup and cold water into another. Let the herb or spice steep (soak) in it for three to four minutes. Remove the tea ball or strainer and taste. Taste both. **Note:** Be careful not to burn yourself with the hot water.

Write a description of the taste:

Hot water: _____

_____

_____

Cold water: _____

_____

_____

Note to teacher: Ground spices dissolve in water. Using them will produce the variety of flavors, but is not an "infusion."

Making Jolly Tea *(cont.)*

Here are some suggestions for words to describe the flavors you are tasting: bitter, sour, spicy, strong, sweet.

Try other herbs and spices and write your descriptions below:

Herb or spice _____
_____

Hot water _____
_____

Cold water _____
_____

Herb or spice _____
_____

Hot water _____
_____

Cold water _____
_____

Herb or spice _____
_____

Hot water _____
_____

Cold water _____
_____

How did water temperature affect the taste of the tea? _____

Did the herb or spice dissolve in the water? _____

What did you learn from this experiment?_____

Which was your favorite flavor?_____

Extensions: Use regular decaffeinated tea bags for the last round and end with a Jolly Tea Party. Provide sugar and/or lemon to add to the tea. Serve with scones made from the recipe on page 69. While using hot water accelerates making tea, it is possible to make "sun tea." Place tea bags in a glass jar of cold water, and put the jar in a window or other sunny spot in the classroom. After several hours observe and taste the tea. Compare the flavor to brewed tea.

Planting Jack's Beanstalk

Learning Objective:

Students will be able to observe and chart the growth of a plant from sprout to adult.

Key Question: What does a plant need to grow?

Teacher Information:

A seed must absorb water before it will sprout and start to grow. A seed has three parts—a seed coat as an outer covering, a small plant, and stored food inside for the small plant. When the seed starts growing, the stem grows up toward the light and the roots grow down toward the pull of gravity. When the first leaves form, the plant begins to make its own food. When plants have what they need (sunlight, water, and minerals from the soil) they grow, make food, and give off oxygen. Environment plays a big part in the proper growth of seeds. In order for plant growth to take place, proper temperature, enough moisture, and air (carbon dioxide) are necessary.

Materials:

- two glass jars with lids
- paper towels
- lima bean seeds
- clear resealable sandwich bags
- masking tape

Procedures:

Students begin their baby plants by making a sprouting bag. First, soak the beans overnight. Fold a paper towel to fit inside a resealable sandwich bag. Dampen it and place five beans on it in the bag. Label each bag with the student's name. Close the bag and tape it to a warm, sunny window.

Have students make Magic Beanstalk Books. Reproduce page 52 and cut along the dashed lines on the outside of the book. Fold in half widthwise along the solid line. Fold in half again along the lengthwise solid line. Students should keep a daily growth log by making sketches or writing descriptions in their Magic Beanstalk Books and by measuring root and stem lengths.

It is a good idea to make extra sprouting bags in case some beans do not germinate. To show the importance of water in seed growth, make one sprouting bag without dampening the paper towel and check it daily.

Measure the seedlings to see how much they grow after two days, four days, six days, and so on. Chart seedling growth on a classroom graph. Do they grow from the top or from the bottom? (top) Mark a spot on the stem and on the foot and see what happens.

Planting Jack's Beanstalk *(cont.)*

Procedures: *(cont.)*

After the seedlings produce leaves, they are ready to be planted. The food stored in the seed is now used up. Plant the seedlings in a cup of potting soil. Be careful not to damage the delicate stems and roots. Carefully poke holes in the bottom of each cup for drainage. Let your students draw a face on the cup and add feet to the bottom to make a plant person. Put the planted cups on plates or pans in a warm, sunny spot, and water each cup with two teaspoons (10 mL) of water daily. Use string to record plant growth. Hold the string beside the plant stem and cut it to match the stem height. Each day, tape the cut string to a poster board chart. Label with the date, and you will have a visual record of your plant's growth.

Extensions:

- Seeds need warmth to sprout. Soak lima beans in water overnight. Dampen two paper towels and use to line each of two jars. Between the glass and the paper, put ten lima beans equally spaced. Cover the jars and place one in a warm place and the other in the refrigerator for five days. Observe the jars each day. Do the seeds in both jars begin to grow? During the cold days of winter, place one jar in a sunny window inside and one in a sunny location outdoors. This is a better test, since both jars would receive sunlight.

- Plants respond to stimuli in the environment. After the seedlings have grown several inches (centimeters) long, ask students what they think will happen if you turn the jar upside down. Turn it over and wait several days, then observe the roots and stems. Are they still upside down? Turn the jar upright and observe it for two more days. What happened? Is this what you thought would happen? Why do you think the roots grow toward the pull of gravity while stems and leaves grow away from gravity? If you plant a seed upside down, will the plant still grow up? (Yes.)

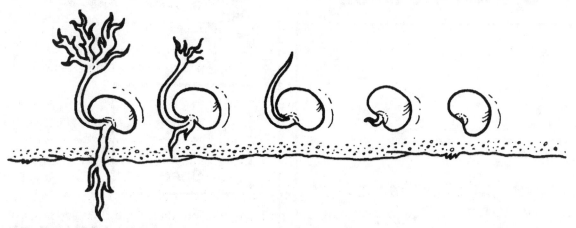

- Plants need materials from the soil, and some types of soil are better for plant growth than others. Plant some of the seedlings in containers with three types of soil such as potting soil, clay, and sand. Give each container the same amount of sunlight and water. Label each container. Have students predict which plant will do best. Chart the results.

- Have students classify seeds by giving them a variety of dried beans and legumes. Have them sort seeds into egg carton cups. Ask students how the seeds are alike and how they are different.

Planting Jack's Beanstalk (cont.)

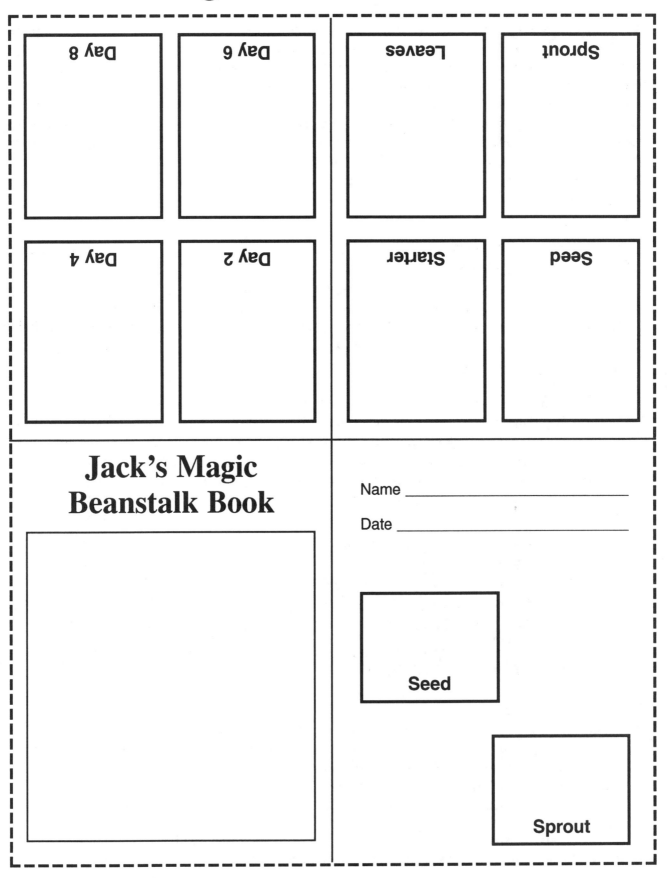

Day 8	**Day 6**
Day 4	**Day 2**

Leaves	**Sprout**
Starter	**Seed**

Jack's Magic Beanstalk Book

Name _____

Date _____

Seed

Sprout

Can Eggs Really Talk?

Different things make different sounds, depending on the density of the items. If the molecules in the item are tightly packed together, this item will be heavier and therefore will produce more sound than items which are lighter and less dense. This simply means the molecules are not as tightly packed together.

In the following experiment, the children will try to identify objects within the eggs by the sounds they make.

Materials:

- Plastic egg
- Egg carton
- Items for eggs: marshmallows, rice, beans, pins, cotton, dice, paper clips, keys, marbles, bottle caps, pennies, toothpicks

Directions:

Plastic eggs are usually available at toy or craft stores, but if they are not available, substitute with film canisters.

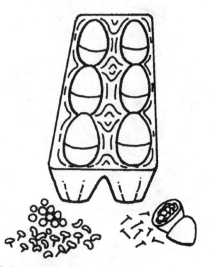

1. Number each egg.

2. Place the items in the plastic eggs and place in egg carton in any order.

3. Have the children close their eyes and listen to the sounds around them. Have the students identify some of the sounds around them. "What do you think makes these sounds different?" "Why are we able to identify one sound from another?"

4. Shake each egg and have the students listen. This is especially fun in small groups where each child can actually shake each egg. Using the handout on the following page, students will predict what is hidden in each egg. Students record their guesses under the pictures of the numbered eggs.

5. Open each egg and show what was inside each one. Students glue the picture of what was actually in each egg on each numbered egg.

Discussion Questions:

1. Which of the objects made a loud sound (the heavier ones or hard ones)?

2. Which ones made a soft sound (the soft or lighter ones)?

3. Which egg made almost no sound?

4. Which object was easier to identify?

5. Were there any other objects you could identify easily? Why?

Can Eggs Really Talk *(cont.)*

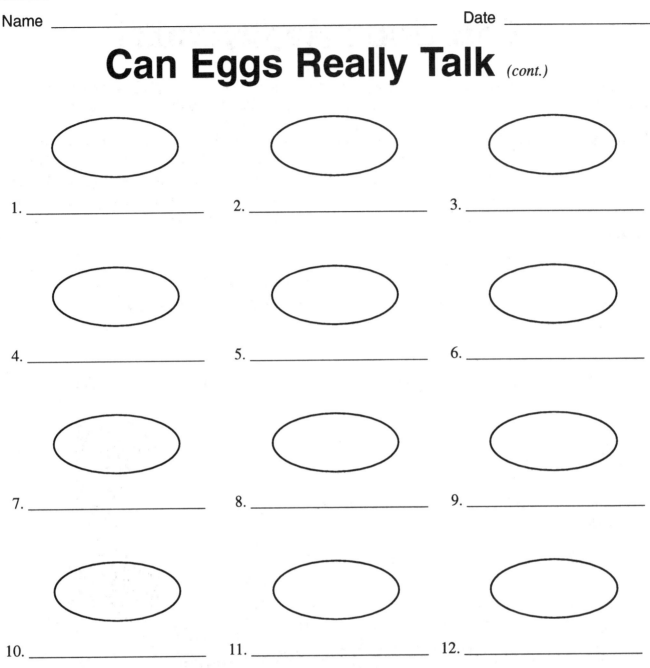

1. _____   2. _____   3. _____

4. _____   5. _____   6. _____

7. _____   8. _____   9. _____

10. _____   11. _____   12. _____

Cut out the pictures. Shake each mystery egg and listen. Guess what is inside each one and write its name underneath the egg. Open the eggs and glue the pictures on the egg to show each sound. How many of your guesses were correct?

Can You See Sound?

Sound is all around. Wind whispering through the trees, birds singing, music playing, and friends laughing are all examples of things that reach our ears as sound.

Sounds are produced when objects vibrate or shake back and forth. These vibrations make the air around the object move. This movement of air is called sound waves. When a sound wave reaches another object, it makes that object vibrate as well. If you could see sound waves, they would look like rounded shapes spreading out from the source of the vibration, like the ripples that spread out when a penny is dropped into a well. Try the observation experiments below to hear and see how sound waves travel.

The Wishing Well Experiment

Materials:

- a large pan of water
- pennies

Directions:

Place the large pan of water on the ground. Stand above the pan and drop one penny at a time into the water.

1. Describe what happens.

2. What do you think causes this to happen?

3. On the back of this page, draw what you see.

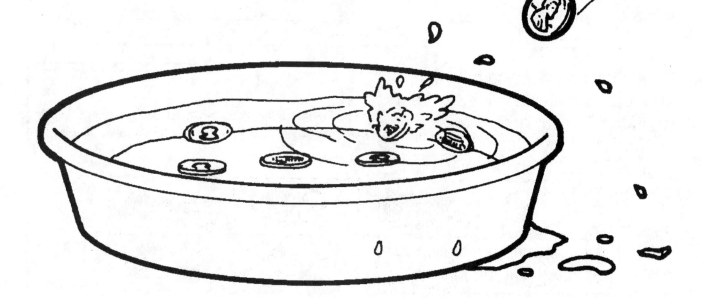

Science

Can You Feel Sound?

When you dropped the penny into the water, you saw waves. You can also see objects vibrate and feel their movement as they produce sound.

Materials:
- tuning fork
- water
- ping pong ball
- tape
- ruler
- rubber band
- thread
- craft stick
- pencil

Directions:

Hold one edge of a ruler tightly against your desk. Pluck the other end of the ruler tightly. Listen.

Describe what you hear. _____

_____

What did you see? _____

_____

Clench the craft stick in your teeth. Pluck the end of the stick and listen. Change the length and try again. _____

_____

What did you hear?_____

_____

What did you feel? _____

_____

Strike a tuning fork and hold it to your ear. Slowly draw it away from and towards your ear. Draw a picture of what you think was happening between the tuning fork and your ear.

Tape a ping pong ball on a thread. While holding the thread, strike the tuning fork and touch the ball with it. Observe what happens. What makes all these activities the same?

Social Studies

Reading a Jolly Map

Use the map to complete the sentences. Remember "Never Eat Soggy Waffles" to help you with directions.

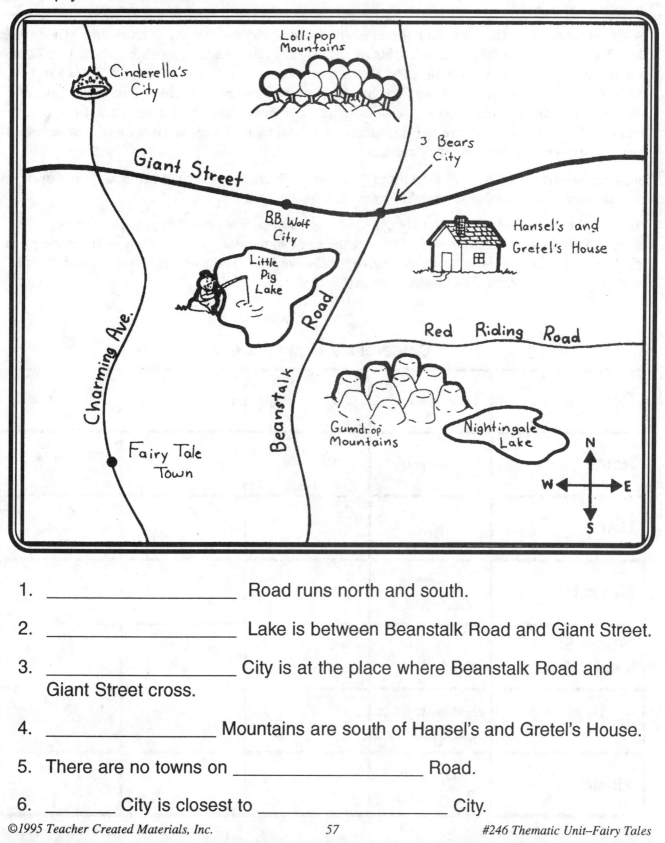

1. _____ Road runs north and south.

2. _____ Lake is between Beanstalk Road and Giant Street.

3. _____ City is at the place where Beanstalk Road and Giant Street cross.

4. _____ Mountains are south of Hansel's and Gretel's House.

5. There are no towns on _____ Road.

6. _____ City is closest to _____ City.

Fairy Tales Around the World

Cinderella, with its theme of "rags to riches," is perhaps the world's best known fairy tale. It has been identified as early as the seventh century in China, and over 900 versions of the story have been collected and indexed.

While all the versions share a basic plot and motif, each has elements unique to its culture. The heroine does not always have a fairy godmother, but there is always some magic. Her slippers may be golden, red, brocade, or ... no slippers at all. The hero is a prince, a pharoah, or even a warrior. They met at the Ball, or the Kabuki theater, or was it a church or a tent? Reading several versions of the Cinderella story can open the door to understanding other cultures. Whether fairy tales have spread from a single source and been modified, or are an expression of universal human needs and emotions, they provide a means to explore and compare many cultures.

See the bibliography on page 79 for a list of "Cinderellas." Enlarge the chart below and fill it in as you read and discuss the similarities and differences among the stories.

Help the children visualize the diversity by using a world map. Cut several slipper shapes from construction paper. As each story is read, write the name of the story or heroine on a slipper and place it on the appropriate country. As an alternative, label a world map on a bulletin board Cinderella, then use string or yarn from the label to each country.

Cinderella's Many Sisters

Country	France			
Name	*Cinderella*			
Hero	*Prince*			
Magic by	*Fairy Godmother*			
Where She Meets Hero	*Ball*			
Test	*Foot must fit in glass slipper*			
Villains	*1 stepmother 2 stepsisters*			

Snow White's Postcard

Materials:

- One 5" x 8" (13 cm x 20 cm) blank index card for each student.
- Copies of the postcard below.

Directions: Students create a message from Snow White to the Seven Dwarfs, telling where she is, what she has seen and thanking them for their help. Write the message on the lines provided.

Address the card to the Seven Dwarfs.

Be sure to add a stamp.

Glue or paste to a blank index card. On the opposite side, draw a picture showing where Snow White and the Prince are now.

Extensions: Make a second postcard and send it through the Jolly Mail to a student on another street in your classroom.

Fairy Tale Jigsaw Puzzle

Draw a scene from a favorite fairy tale. Be sure to color everything and add detail. Cut on the lines and give the pieces to a friend to put together again.

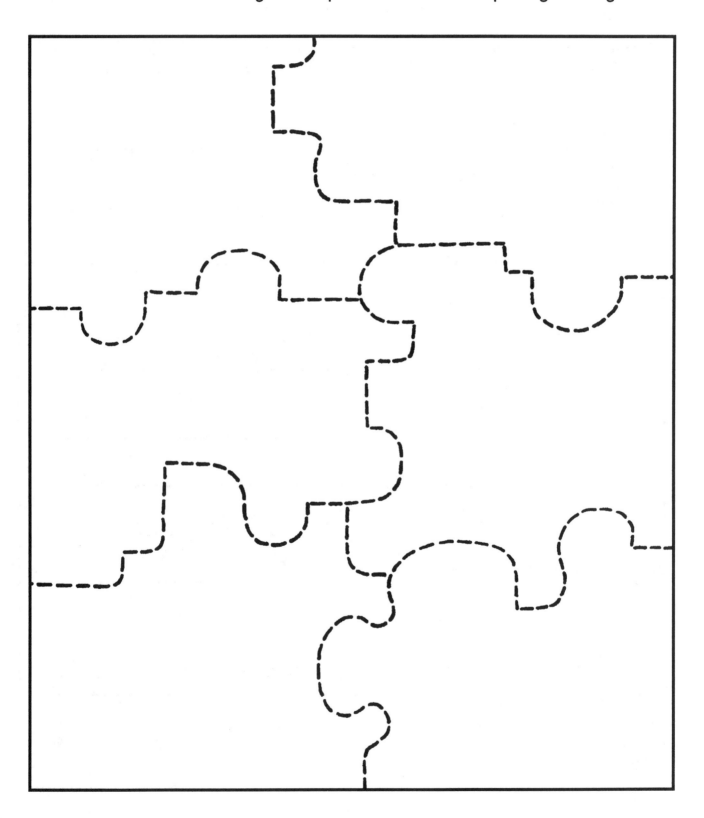

60

Pop-up Greeting Card

Design a get well pop-up card by following the directions below.

Materials: 2 pieces of 9" x 12" (23 cm x 30 cm) paper per card; glue; crayons, colored pencils, or markers; picture drawn by student or cut from magazine

Directions

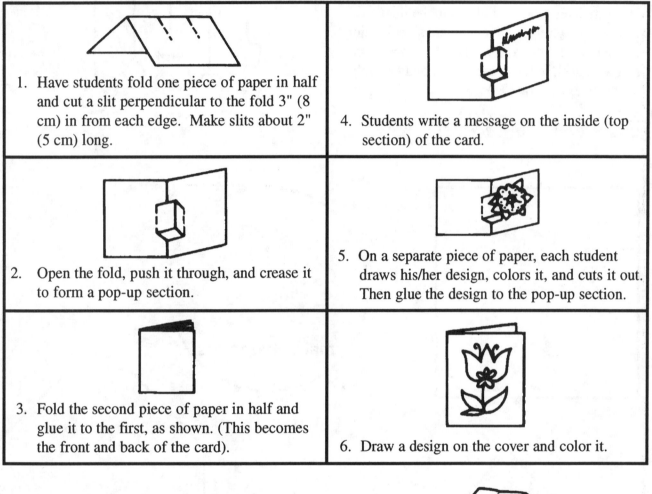

1. Have students fold one piece of paper in half and cut a slit perpendicular to the fold 3" (8 cm) in from each edge. Make slits about 2" (5 cm) long.

2. Open the fold, push it through, and crease it to form a pop-up section.

3. Fold the second piece of paper in half and glue it to the first, as shown. (This becomes the front and back of the card).

4. Students write a message on the inside (top section) of the card.

5. On a separate piece of paper, each student draws his/her design, colors it, and cuts it out. Then glue the design to the pop-up section.

6. Draw a design on the cover and color it.

Design a Gingerbread House

Materials:

- small milk cartons
- canned frosting
- graham crackers
- plastic knives
- assorted candies
- sturdy paper plates

Directions: Give each child six squares of graham crackers, one very clean small milk carton (a little bleach in the wash water helps), and one plastic knife. Place the milk carton on a sturdy paper plate. Using the frosting as mortar, students cover the sides and top of the carton with graham crackers. Fill any empty spaces with frosting. Decorate the houses by attaching assorted small candies with icing.

Fairy Tale Mobile

Materials:

- wire coat hangers
- string or yarn

Directions:

Have students label and illustrate the main characters, setting, minor characters, and major problem of their favorite fairy tale on the cutouts below. Punch holes in each piece and tie to the coat hanger as shown.

Hang completed mobiles around the room.

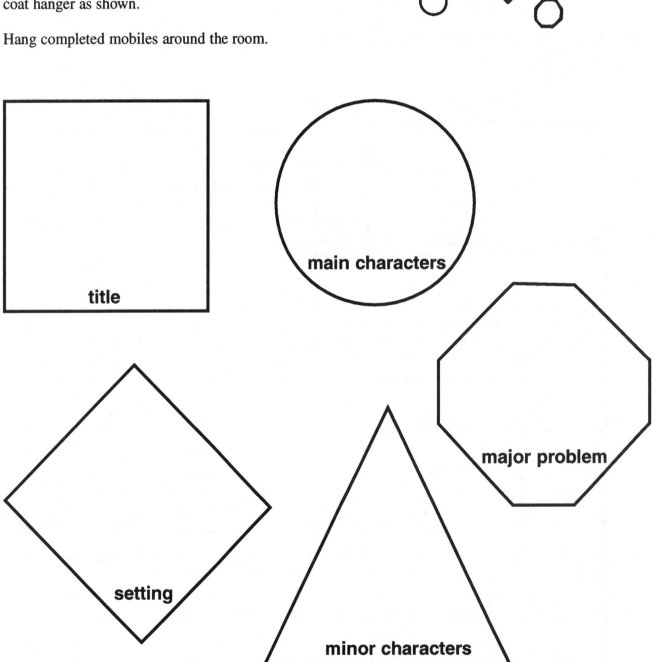

title

main characters

major problem

setting

minor characters

Cinderella's Castle

Castles are usually built out of stone or bricks, so they are strong and protect the people who live inside them.

By combining basic shapes, you can create a castle of your own. Cut out the shapes and glue them together on a piece of construction paper. Start with a square, then add some rectangles as towers. The roofs are made of triangles. Use smaller rectangles as windows and squares to complete the top and as the door. Draw circles for stone walls or rectangles for bricks. If you wish, use a small triangle as a flag on the tower.

Teacher's Note: Older students may be able to use an arched shape for windows and doors.

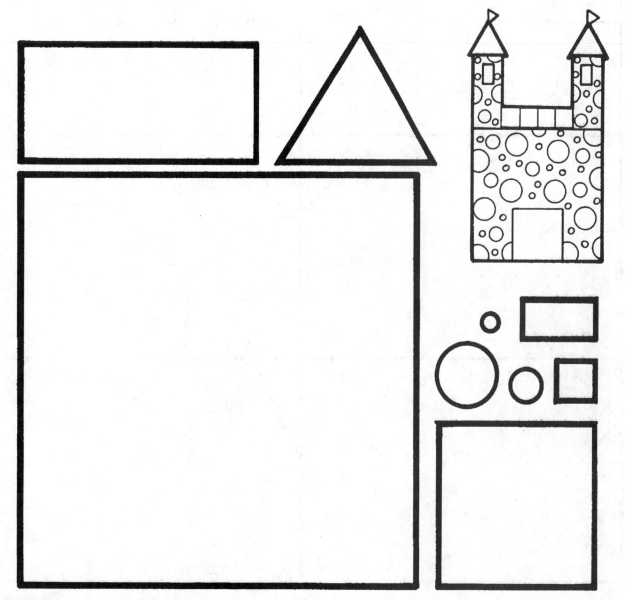

Create a Fairy Tale

Make up your own fairy tale. Include the characters you have just read about, then create some of your own. Remember, in the magical world of charms and spells, anything can happen! Be sure to use story elements from the fairy tale recipe.

When you have finished creating your story, draw it out on the panels below. Give it a title. Cut the pages out and staple them together to have your own story book.

Extension: Using the stories create a Big Book for your classroom.

My Story _____ By _____ 1	4
2	5
3	6

Create a Stamp

Every piece of mail must have a postage stamp, which shows that a fee has been paid to cover the cost of delivering the mail. The amount paid is indicated on the stamp. There is also a design. Some stamps have pictures of famous people, while others have pictures of flowers, special designs, and seasonal or patriotic pictures.

Stamp art is so special that contests are held to pick new designs, and some people collect different stamps.

In the space below, design a stamp to use in the Jolly Post Office. Choose a character or event from one of our stories. How much does the stamp cost? Be sure to include the price.

Extension: Have students bring in stamps from mail their families have received. Mount them for sharing or use them to form collages.

Using Sound to Create a Classroom Band

Teacher's Note: If possible, bring a variety of instruments into the classroom and demonstrate how they work to produce sound. Explore the different ways sound is produced by making the musical instruments on the following pages. Use them during singing time to create a classroom band.

Sound is produced through vibrations. The more something vibrates, the stronger the sound that is produced. Musical instruments work in much the same way. Blowing, striking, or plucking an instrument causes the air surrounding it to move. These sound waves produce pleasant sounds we call music.

Plucking Instruments

Rubber Band

Materials: variety of rubber bands

Directions: Have children work as partners. Let one take a rubberband and stretch it in his or her fingers. Have the other child pluck the rubber band to create music.

Shoe Box Guitar

Materials: shoe box with lid, assorted rubber bands, scissors

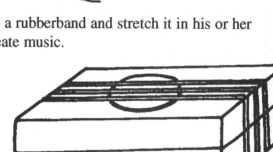

Directions: Cut a hole in the lid of a shoe box. Stretch different width rubber bands lengthwise around the box, over the hole.

To Play: Pluck bands singly or together. The narrow bands will have a high sound; the wide bands will have a low sound.

Striking Instruments

Drums

Materials: oatmeal box, coffee can, ice cream container or margarine tub; balloon; rubber band; pencil

Directions: A clean oatmeal box, margarine container, ice cream container or coffee can, with a lid, makes a drum.

To Play: Strike the drum head (lid or balloon) with the eraser end of a pencil.

As an alternative, especially for older children, stretch a balloon over the open end of a coffee can or large tin can. Put a rubber band around the top to hold the balloon tightly over the can.

66

Using Sound to Create a Classroom Band *(cont.)*

Glass Bottle

Materials: Variety of glass bottles, water

Directions: Get several glass bottles and fill with water to different heights.

To Play: Either strike the bottles with a pencil or blow across the mouth of the bottles. The bottles will have different pitches depending on how much water is in the bottle.

Clay Flower Pot

Materials: clay flower pots, string, dowel, pencil

Directions: Thread a string through the drainage hole in the pot and knot it or tie a small piece of wood dowel to it. Hold the pot by the string and strike with a pencil to produce a nice bell tone.

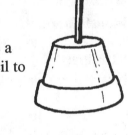

Tambourine

Materials: two aluminum pie pans or paper plates, beans or seeds, tape or staples

Directions: Place several beans or seeds in one tin. Put the second tin face down on top of the one with the beans and tape or staple them together.

To Play: Strike the bottom of the pan with one hand or shake the pans.

Maracas

Materials: clean dry soda can, seeds or pebbles, unsharpened wood pencil, tape, hammer and nail

Directions: Put several seeds or pebbles in each can and place tape over the open end. Have an adult punch a hole in the center of the bottom of each can and push an unsharpened pencil through the bottom hole. Poke the end of the pencil through the hole on the top of the can, so that it sticks out no more than ¹/₂ inch (1.3 cm). Secure ends of the pencil with tape.

To Play: Holding the pencil, shake the can rhythmically.

Using Sound to Create a Classroom Band *(cont.)*

Blowing Instruments

Straw Flute and Trumpet

Materials: drinking straw; paper cup, scissors

Directions: Flatten the first 2 inches (5 cm) on the straw. Snip off the corners of the flattened end with scissors.

To Play: Blow into straw to make a flute-like sound. The pitch of the flute will depend on the length of the straw.

To make a straw trumpet, prepare the straw the same way, but insert the straw into the bottom of a paper cup.

Comb Kazoo

Materials: hair comb, rubber band, wax paper, scissors

Directions: Wrap wax paper around a comb and fasten it with a rubber band.

To Play: Hold the kazoo up to your lips and hum gently while pursing your lips and letting them vibrate against the paper.

Tube Kazoo

Materials: toilet tissue or paper towel tube; scissors; wax paper; rubber band

Directions: Cover one end of the tube with a 4" (10 cm) square of wax paper. Use rubber band to hold paper in place. Punch three holes in a row, about 1" (2.5 cm) apart, lengthwise along one side of the tube.

To Play: Blow into tube. Change notes by covering and uncovering the holes with fingers.

Design Your Own Instrument

Design a new instrument. It should make sound when you strike it, blow through it, or pluck it. Draw a picture of your instrument. Label its parts. Write directions on how to make your musical instrument. Describe the sound your instrument makes. Explain why it works.

Fairy Tale Recipes

Jolly Postman Scones

Scones are a favorite treat in England and throughout the United Kingdom. The Jolly Postman might enjoy either of these recipes with his tea as he visits the inhabitants of the countryside.

Oven Scones

Ingredients

- 2 cups (50 g) sifted all-purpose flour
- 2½ (12.5 mL) teaspoons baking powder
- ¼ teaspoon (1.25 mL) baking soda
- 1 tablespoon (15 mL) salt
- 1 tablespoon (15mL) sugar
- ¼ cup (63 mL) butter or margarine
- 1 egg, well beaten
- ⅔ cup (170 mL) buttermilk
- ½ cup (125 mL) raisins (optional)

Directions

Mix flour, baking powder, baking soda, salt, and sugar in a bowl. Cut in shortening with a pastry blender or rub in with your fingertips until crumbly. Mix in egg and buttermilk. Turn dough out on a lightly floured board and pat out in a circle about ½ inch (1.27 cm) thick. Prick all over with a fork. Cut in wedges. Place wedges on a baking sheet. Bake at 450°F (230°C) for 10–15 minutes. Serve with butter and jam or honey. Serves 12.

Drop Scones

Ingredients

- 2 cups (500 mL) all-purpose flour
- 1½ teaspoons (8 mL) baking powder
- ¼ teaspoon (1.25 mL) baking soda
- ½ teaspoon (2.5 mL) salt
- 1½ cups (375 mL) thick buttermilk
- 1 egg, beaten
- 2 tablespoons (30 mL) sugar

Directions

Mix flour, salt, sugar, baking powder, and baking soda in a bowl. Stir in egg and buttermilk. Batter will be like pancake batter.

Pour batter in 2" (5 cm) rounds on a medium-hot, lightly greased griddle. Cook scones until they are lightly browned on the underside and covered with small bubbles on top. Turn and cook the other side. Place in folded towel until ready to serve. Serve hot or cold with butter and jam or honey.

Fairy Tale Recipes *(cont.)*

Gingerbread Boys And Girls

The children will enjoy decorating and eating these gingerbread boys and girls, which are a favorite treat not only of the English but children all across Europe.

Ingredients

- 2¼ cups (560 mL) flour
- ½ cup (125 mL) butter or margarine
- 10 tablespoons (150 mL) dark brown sugar
- 2 teaspoons (10 mL) ground ginger
- pinch ground cinnamon
- decorator's icing
- a little water

Directions

Put flour and spices into mixing bowl and mix in the butter, until mixture resembles fine breadcrumbs. Stir in the sugar, using a little water, and mix to a firm dough. Roll out on a lightly floured board to about ¼ inch (.6 cm) thick, and use a gingerbread man cutter to cut out cookies. Place on a greased cookie sheet and bake at 325° F (170ºC) for about 15–20 minutes. Cool on a wire rack. Pipe on faces and buttons with decorator's icing.

Red Riding Hood Shortbread

Although shortbread originated with the Scots, it is now enjoyed throughout the United Kingdom during tea time and holidays. Children can imagine this might have been just the sort of treat Red Riding Hood was bringing to Grandma. This recipe serves 20.

Ingredients

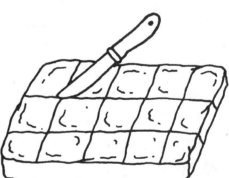

- 1 cup (250 mL) butter
- ½ cup plus 2 tablespoons (155 mL) sugar
- 2 cups (500 mL) sifted all purpose flour
- ¼ teaspoon (1 mL) salt
- ¼ teaspoon (1 mL) baking powder

Directions

Beat butter until light and creamy. Beat in ½ cup of sugar. Sift the flour, salt, and baking powder together and fold into butter mixture. Place dough on a cookie sheet and pat into a rectangle, ½" (1.2 cm) thick and approximately 4" x 10" (10 x 25.4 cm) in size. Sprinkle remaining sugar over top and bake in the center of a preheated 350⁰ F (180⁰ C) oven for 15 minutes until edges are lightly browned. Cut into bars and serve.

Fun and Games

Fairy Tale Tag

In this simple game of tag, children are paired in twos. On a deck of cards, write the names of the fairy tale characters listed below. Before play begins, each child must find his or her partner by matching his/her character with a character from the same fairy tale.

Cinderella/Fairy Godmother	Snow White/the Dwarves
Goldilocks/Baby Bear	Mirror/Snow White's Stepmother
Red Riding Hood/Grandma	The Gingerbread Boy/the Old Woman
Jack/the Giant	First Little Pig/Second Little Pig
Hansel/Gretel	Hansel's and Gretel's Stepmother/Hansel's and
Elves/Shoemaker	Gretel's Father
Beauty/the Beast	Big Billy Goat Gruff/Little Billy Goat Gruff

Directions: This tag game can be played in a large group or with as few as two children. One child in each pair is designated "It," while the other partner has to keep from being tagged. All children are moving constantly.

Play begins with a signal from the teacher (a whistle or special word). If the child who is "It" tags his/her partner, the partner becomes "It." Play continues for any teacher specified time.

Fairy Tale Switch

Have everyone find a partner in the manner listed above. On your signal, each pair walks about a designated area, the back person following the front person. When you say the name of a fairy tale and the word "Switch" (e.g., Jack and the Beanstalk switch!), everyone does an about-face (turns around) and the game continues with the other partner leading. When you say the word "Rotate," the back person moves ahead to be the front person. Repeat several times and mix up your commands. The game can be changed to include groups of three or even four.

Giants, Wizards, and Elves

This is similar to "Rock, Paper, and Scissors." Giants raise their arms above their heads and make a giant "AAAAAAAH" sound. Wizards bend their knees and shake their hands out straight in front of them, as if casting a spell and Wizards say, "OOOOOOH!" Elves bend their knees, open their arms out to the side and yell, "EEEEEEEH!"

Giants can crush Wizards, Wizards can cast a spell on Elves, and Elves can trip Giants. Divide students into two equal groups. Each group decides which character they will all be and forms a line side by side, facing the opposing team. On your signal, the groups display their character, and, depending on their combination, will either chase or flee until the signal to end the round is given. A tagged player sits out one round.

Fairy Tale Ball

Cinderella met the Prince at the ball, and Blanche attended many grand parties after she moved to the city. To end the unit and synthesize learning, use some or all of these ideas to plan a grand Fairy Tale Ball.

* Encourage children to come dressed as their favorite fairy tale characters.

* Use the letter on page 73 to remind parents and to solicit help with the Ball.

* Make invitations using the pop-up card pattern and invite parents and/or other guests to attend the Ball.

* Children will enjoy doing the Virginia Reel and other simple folk dances as part of the Ball.

* Refreshments may include results of the tea infusion experiment. Make real tea using decaffeinated tea bags, and make sugar, milk and/or lemon available, or use tea as the basis for a fruit juice punch.

* Make scones, shortbread, or gingerbread men as a class project or ask children to bring samples of the treats they shared in the class cookbook.

* Have students serve the refreshments, rotating jobs so that everyone has an opportunity to pour or serve.

* For entertainment, present "Jack and the Beanstalk Reader's Theater" (pages 35–37).

* Have the children use the instruments they have made to accompany themselves in singing.

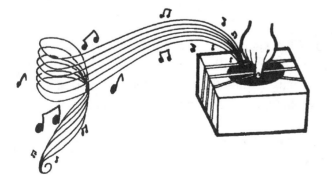

Dear Parents,

We would like to celebrate all of our learning and culminate our unit by holding a Fairy Tale Ball on _____.

For the ball, your child should dress as his or her favorite fairy tale character.

We would appreciate your help in providing for this festive occasion. We will need help with decorating and refreshments and a few parents to assist on the day of the Ball. Please check below if you would like to help with this project.

- -

Tear off and return.

I can provide…

_____ punch

_____ cookies

_____ napkins

_____ cups

_____ my time from _____ to _____ .

_____ I can help at the ball.

_____ I will provide decorating services.

Parent's Name _____

Child's Name _____

Phone # _____ Best time to call me _____

Once again, we would like to thank you for your help.

Sincerely,

Letter Writing Center

Provide a learning center for students who wish to write letters. Post samples of different types of letters—business letters, personal letters, etc. Make available index cards for postcards, an assortment of letterhead paper, using headings on page 76 and stationery on page 77, and envelopes or copies of the envelope pattern on page 75. Include stickers to use as stamps and glue and/or tape for putting things together. Encourage students to write to classmates, fairy tale characters, or families.

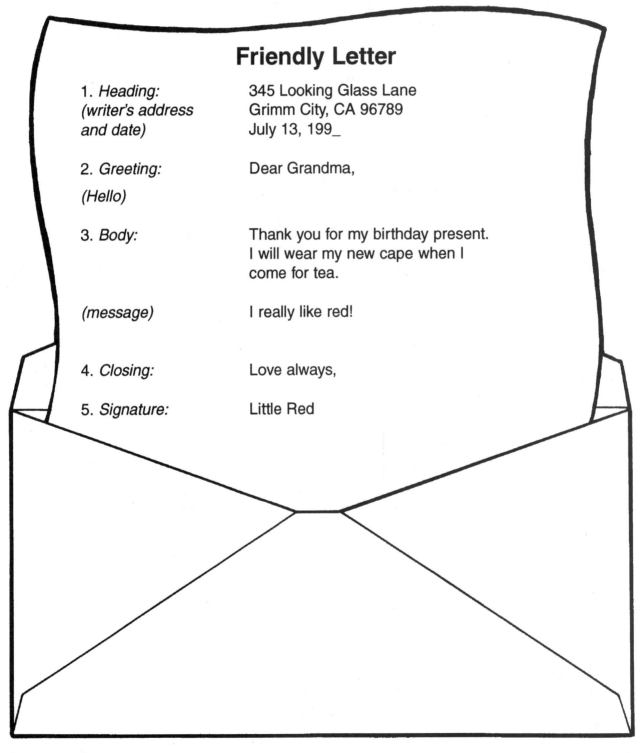

Friendly Letter

1. *Heading:*
   (writer's address
   and date)

   345 Looking Glass Lane
   Grimm City, CA 96789
   July 13, 199_

2. *Greeting:*
   (Hello)

   Dear Grandma,

3. *Body:*

   Thank you for my birthday present.
   I will wear my new cape when I
   come for tea.

   (message)

   I really like red!

4. *Closing:*

   Love always,

5. *Signature:*

   Little Red

Envelopes

1. Cut on solid lines.

2. Fold tabs A to the back on the dotted lines.

3. Fold tab B to the back and paste or glue it to the A s.

4. Address your envelope and insert your letter.

5. Fold tab C over to close the envelope. Seal it with tape or a sticker.

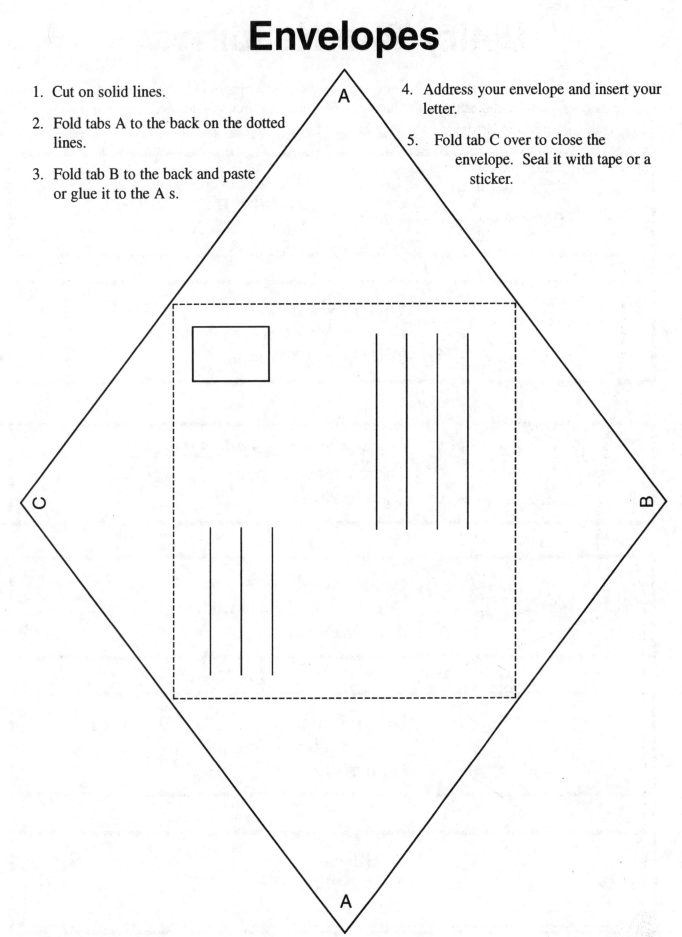

#246 Thematic Unit–Fairy Tales

Fairy Tale Headings

Teacher's Note: Use these creative headings with the handout on page 77 to create letterhead stationery for a variety of letter writing activities. Make it available to children in your letter writing center.

The Three Little Pigs
The Brick House
Windy Forest Road, The Woods

Wicked Witch
Gingerbread Cottage
The Haunted Woods

Mr. And Mrs. Bear And Baby
Three Bears Cottage
The Woods

Mr. V. Bigg
Top Of The Beanstalk
Jack's Farm

B.B. Wolf Esq.
C/O Grandma's Cottage
Horner's Corner

Goldilocks
24 Blackbird Road
Banbury Cross

Letterhead Stationery

Glue heading here.

Parent Letter

Dear Parents,

We have been studying *The Jolly Postman or Other People's Letters*, a book about a postman who delivers letters and packages to various fairy tale characters. Along with this study, we are reading other fairy tales, studying the post office, and working with infusion and sound in science.

As an added treat for our classroom, we would like to put together a Jolly Postman Recipe Book. Your child should choose his/her favorite cookie or treat recipe, name it after a fairy tale character, and write it on the card provided below (e.g., Jack and the Beanstalk Brownies, Cinderella Shortbread, or Three Bears Toffee Bars). We will bind our recipes into a book for your child to take home.

Thank you,

Bibliography

Fairy Tales

Ahlberg, Janet and Allan. *The Jolly Postman or Other People's Letters*. Little, Brown, and Co., 1986.

Ai-Ling, Louis. *Yeh-Shen: A Cinderella Story from China*. Philomel, 1982.

Brett, Jan. *Goldilocks and the Three Bears*. G.P. Putnam's Sons, 1987.

Brothers Grimm. *Grimm's Fairy Tales*. Grosset and Dunlap, 1991.

Climo, Shirley. *The Egyptian Cinderella*. Harper Trophy, 1989.

Climo, Shirley. *The Korean Cinderella*. Harper Collins, 1993.

de la Paz, Myrna. *Abadeha, The Phillipine Cinderella*. Pazific Queen, 1991.

Espinosa, J. Manuel. *Folklore of Spain in the American Southwest*. University of Oklahoma Press, 1985.

Howe, John. *Jack and the Beanstalk*. Little, Brown, and Co., 1989.

Martin, Rafe. *Rough-faced Girl* (Algonquin Indian). Putnam, 1992.

Roberts, Tom. *Red Riding Hood*. Rabbit Ears Publications, 1991.

San Souci, Robert D. *The Talking Eggs*. Scholastic, 1989.

Scieszka, Jon. *The True Story of the Three Little Pigs*. Scholastic, Inc., 1989.

Seki, Keigo. *Fairy Tales of Japan*. (translated by Robert J. Adams) University of Chicago Press, 1963.

Steptoe, John. *Mufaro's Beautiful Daughters* (Africa). Lothrop, 1987.

Vuong, Lynette Dyer. *The Brocaded Slipper and Other Vietnamese Tales*. Harper Trophy, 1992.

Winthrop, Elizabeth. *Vasilissa, The Beautiful* (Russia). Harper Trophy, 1991.

Wood, Audrey. *Quick as a Cricket*. Child's Play (International) Ltd., 1982.

Background Information

Cobb, Vicki. *More Science Experiments You Can Eat*. Scholastic, Inc., 1979.

Gibbons, Gail. *The Post Office Book: Mail and How It Moves*. Thomas Y. Crowell, 1982.

Jennings, Terry. *The Young Scientist Investigates Sound*. Children's Press, 1982.

Poetry

McNaughton, Colin. *Who's Been Sleeping in My Porridge?* Ideals Children's Books, 1990.

Audio

Ahlberg, Janet. *The Jolly Postman or Other People's Letters* (read by Tim Curry and Andrea Martin). Harper Collins, 1993.

Folk Dances for Fun. RCA Victor, 1958.

Prokofiev, Sergey. *Peter and the Wolf*. (Benjamin Britten narrates.) New York

Special Folk Dances. (includes directions) RCA Victor, 1958.

Answer Key

Page 16

1. 4
2. 2
3. 1
4. 6
5. 3
6. 5

Page 28

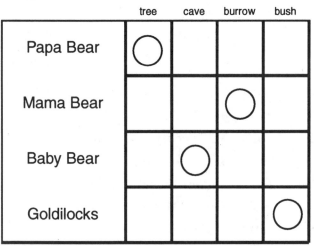

Page 42

1. 16 miles
2. 17 miles
3. 28 miles
4. 13 miles
5. 46 miles

Page 43

1. $1.37
2. $0.70
3. $0.36
4. $0.48
5. One letter and one postcard
6. $3.62

Page 47

1. 20 chickens
2. 36 rabbits
3. 36 eggs
4. 9 diamonds
5. 14 eggs
6. 7 rabbits

Page 56

1-3. Various written answers.

4. You can see, feel, and hear the effects of vibrations.

Page 57

1. Beanstalk Road
2. Little Pig Lake
3. 3 Bears City
4. Gumdrop Mountains
5. Red Riding Road
6. 3 Bears City is closest to B.B. Wolf City